CW01509482

THE POCKET

DISCOVER
LONDON

G:

Published in 2025
by Gemini Gift Books
Part of Gemini Books Group

Based in Woodbridge and London

Marine House, Tide Mill Way,
Woodbridge, Suffolk IP12 1AP
United Kingdom
www.geminibooks.com

Text and Design © 2025 Gemini Gift Books Ltd
Part of the Gemini Pockets series

Text by Becky Freeth

Cover illustration by Grace Helmer

ISBN 978-1-80247-304-9

All rights reserved. No part of this publication may be reproduced in any form or by any means – electronic, mechanical, photocopying, recording or otherwise – or stored in any retrieval system of any nature without prior written permission from the copyright holders.

A CIP catalogue record for this book is available from the British Library.

Disclaimer: The book is a guidebook purely for information and entertainment purposes only. All trademarks, individual and company names, brand names, registered names, quotations, celebrity names, logos, dialogues and catchphrases used or cited in this book are the property of their respective owners. The publisher does not assume and hereby disclaims any liability to any party for any loss, damage or disruption caused by errors or omissions, whether such errors or omissions result from negligence, accident or any other cause. This book is an unofficial and unauthorized publication by Gemini Adult Books Ltd and has not been licensed, approved, sponsored or endorsed by any other person or entity.

Manufacturer's EU Representative: Eurolink Compliance Limited, 25 Herbert Place, Dublin, D02 AY86, Republic of Ireland. admin@eurolink-europe.ie

Printed in China

10 9 8 7 6 5 4 3 2 1

MIX
Paper | Supporting
responsible forestry
FSC® C020056
www.fsc.org

Image credits: Shutterstock: 4 / Fajar Adinda Putra; 24 / netsign33; 28 / JeanneLolness; 30 / RomanYa; 32, 36 / HENX; 40, 41 / Alunal; 56, 57, 72, 73, 86, 87 / NEGOVURA31; 70 / nikiteev_konstantin; 108 / Tetiana Bihus; 112 / Odin Illustration; 122, 123 / 19srb81. Julyan Bayes: 63, 83, 115, 127. Freepik: 23, 47, 88, 92, 111; 6, 11, 13, 15, 17, 19, 21, 27, 84, 122, 123 / Nenilkime; 66 / macrovector; 97, 104 / Natanaelginting.

THE
POCKET

DISCOVER
LONDON

G:

CONTENTS

Welcome to London: land of red buses and black taxis. Big Ben, Buckingham Palace and Tower Bridge. Icons of British culture.

Whether you have a day in the capital, a week, or more, there are so many things you must see and do. Visit a real palace. Wander through one of the world-class art galleries or hunt for a Banksy. Travel on the underground. Drink a pint in a London pub. Stay for Sunday lunch. Dress up for afternoon tea, then take in a West End show.

Let this pocket guide be your introduction to the best this city has to offer – and live like a Londoner!

"London is a collection of villages, each with its own character and charm."

Roy Ayers

Did You Know?

London has four unmissable UNESCO World Heritage sites:

* Palace of Westminster and Westminster Abbey, including St Margaret's Church
* Tower of London
* Maritime Greenwich
* Royal Botanic Gardens, Kew

CENTRAL LONDON

HIGHLIGHTS

Hyde Park
National Gallery
Houses of Parliament
Buckingham Palace
Kensington Palace
Westminster Abbey

AREAS TO EXPLORE

Covent Garden, Soho,
Mayfair, Kensington & Chelsea

FREE EXPERIENCES

✳ Soak up the Strand, home to the
   most famous West End shows

✳ Explore bustling
   Piccadilly Circus

✳ Visit the Science Museum

✳ Tour Tate Britain

✳ Walk through Chinatown

✳ View Nelson's Column and the
   lions in Trafalgar Square

NORTH LONDON

HIGHLIGHTS

Alexandra Palace
London Zoo
British Museum
Regent's Canal
Madame Tussauds
Hampstead Heath
Camden Lock

AREAS TO EXPLORE

Hampstead, Camden Town,
Primrose Hill

FREE EXPERIENCES

* ❋ Recreate the Beatles'
famous album cover outside
Abbey Road Studios
* ❋ Explore Camden Market
* ❋ Visit the Amy Winehouse bronze
statue in Stables Market
* ❋ Tour the British Museum
* ❋ Pay homage to famous names
at Highgate Cemetery

EAST LONDON

HIGHLIGHTS

Brick Lane
Old Spitalfields Market
Queen Elizabeth Olympic Park
London Museum Docklands
Victoria Park

AREAS TO EXPLORE

Shoreditch, Spitalfields, Whitechapel

FREE EXPERIENCES

❊ Sunday morning shopping at Columbia Road Flower Market

❊ Vintage treasure hunting at Old Spitalfields

❊ Nature walk in Victoria Park near Tower Hamlets

❊ Window-shopping at BOXPARK, Shoreditch

THE CITY

HIGHLIGHTS

St Paul's Cathedral
Museum of London
Tower of London
Sky Garden
Monument to the Great
Fire of London

AREAS TO EXPLORE

Clerkenwell, Canary Wharf

FREE EXPERIENCES

* Explore London's largest collection of free art, including the Traffic Light Tree outside Billingsgate Market
* Picnic at Jubilee Park, a green oasis in a concrete jungle
* Walk the route of the Great Fire of London from Monument Station to St Paul's Cathedral

SOUTH LONDON

HIGHLIGHTS

Shakespeare's Globe
Royal Observatory
Old Royal Naval College
London Eye
Tower of London
O2 Arena
Cutty Sark Museum
London Dungeon
Sea Life

AREAS TO EXPLORE

Greenwich, Southwark, South Bank, Bermondsey, Bankside

FREE EXPERIENCES

* Sightseeing on the South Bank
* Hunt for Banksy's *Girl with Balloon* artwork on Waterloo Bridge
* Explore the reimagined Battersea Power Station
* Wander the grounds of the ornate Old Royal Naval College

WEST LONDON

HIGHLIGHTS

Kensington Palace
Design Museum
Royal Albert Hall
Holland Park

AREAS TO EXPLORE

Notting Hill, Bayswater,
Maida Vale, South Kensington

FREE EXPERIENCES

✻ Kyoto Garden in Holland Park

✻ Experience the Design Museum
on the corner of Holland Park

✻ Photograph the colourful
houses in Notting Hill

✻ Discover the fabulously
floral Churchill Arms pub

CHAPTER ONE

SIGHT
SEEING

Buckingham Palace

**BEST FOR: HISTORY OF THE ROYALS
AREA: CITY OF WESTMINSTER
(OPEN SUMMER)**

Don't Miss... Afternoon tea at one of the world's most famous homes. Runs July to September in the Garden Café.

Did You Know... Inside this royal residence, there's a post office, police station, cinema and health clinic.

Insider Tip... Book the earliest ticket of the day to combine your visit with lunch in the grounds.

Step inside an iconic British palace so rich in royal history that it should be top of any visit-London bucket list.

The magnificent 775-room palace has been home to reigning British monarchs – including Queen Elizabeth II and her father King George VI – since 1837.

The sumptuous State Rooms in which Queen Victoria once hosted balls with music by Mendelssohn, and where the Prince and Princess of Wales posed for their official wedding photos, have been open to the viewing public for the last 30 years.

Visitors can also snoop inside the decadent room where King Charles' throne now sits beneath five breath-taking cut-glass chandeliers.

Royal Residents of Buckingham Palace

1837
Queen Victoria is the first sovereign to rule from Buckingham Palace.

1901
After moving in, King Edward VII hosts many social occasions here with Queen Alexandra.

1935
King George V and Queen Mary give the home a Regency makeover during his reign.

1940
During World War II, when the palace is bombed five times in one night, King George VI is living here with Queen Elizabeth I.

1948
The Music Room is converted into a medical theatre for the birth of King Charles III.

1952
Queen Elizabeth moves into the Palace with Prince Philip when she ascends the throne.

"It is not the walls that make the city, but the people who live within them. The walls of London may be battered, but the spirit of the Londoner stands resolute and undismayed."

King George VI's radio address from an air raid shelter underneath Buckingham Palace after the World War II bombings in September 1940

The Tower of London

BEST FOR: HORRIBLE HISTORY
AREA: TOWER HILL

Don't Miss... The iconic Beefeater guards in full regalia at each entrance.

Did You Know... Notorious London gangsters the Kray Twins were among the last to be imprisoned here, in 1952.

Insider Tip... Make the Jewel House your first stop as it's the most popular and busiest attraction.

Welcome to the dark side of London's long and winding history. An imposing fortress on the River Thames, the Tower of London has been both a home to ancient royals and a terrifying place of execution. Three of Henry VIII's ill-fated wives lived and died at the castle.

For many years, it served as a secure prison – excellent preparation for the job it holds today: protecting England's 800-year-old Crown Jewels. Paired with the intrigue of the Tower's gruesome past, the collection of sceptres, orbs and crowns from English coronations make this the capital's most-visited paid attraction.

According to legend, there are always six ravens present in the Tower of London.

Tower Bridge

BEST FOR: VIEWS OF THE RIVER THAMES
AREA: BERMONDSEY

Don't Miss... The lifting of the bascules, which happens around 800 times a year.

Did You Know... In 1952, a red double-decker bus once accelerated over the bridge as it was opening, after a warning signal failed to go off. No-one was hurt.

Insider Tip... Combine your tour ticket with the Tower of London to tick off two incredible landmarks.

If your wobbly knees will carry you, walking the 140-ft (42-m) high glass platform is an unforgettable way to see Tower Bridge raise its bascules for a river boat.

The bascules (two sides of the bridge) used to go up and down 6,000 times a year when it was first opened in 1894, then powered exclusively by steam. Today, you have to be in the right place at the right time to witness this remarkable feat of engineering.

Your best chance? Enter at the northwest tower and take a guided tour across the top. At the south tower, enjoy an in-depth exploration of the inner mechanisms in the Engine Room.

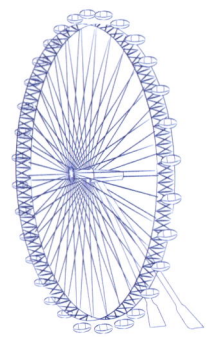

London Eye

BEST FOR: A DAYTIME DATE
AREA: SOUTH BANK

Don't Miss... A glimpse of Windsor Castle
(23 miles/37 km away) on a clear day.

Did You Know... You can pay extra for
an exclusive "Cupid's Pod" for two.

Insider Tip... Avoid peak times: 11 am–3 pm.

What could be more romantic than floating over London's incredible cityscape in your own glass bubble? It's perhaps why the London Eye has witnessed more than 5,000 marriage proposals.

Amazingly, the 443-ft (135-m) high Ferris wheel (once the largest in the world) was only ever meant to stay on the Thames for five years; but it has been so popular that it still stands two decades later, attracting around 3.5 million tourists every year.

Best City Views

Primrose Hill, Regent's Park
For city skyline sunsets

IFS Cloud Cable Car
For aerial views of Canary Wharf

Parliament Hill, Hampstead Heath
London's highest natural viewpoint

The View from The Shard
40-mile (64-km) 360-degree views

Sky Garden at The Fenchurch Building
Try yoga in the clouds

Roof Terrace at One New Change
For cocktails overlooking St Paul's

Waterloo Bridge
For glorious views of the River Thames

"There's nowhere else like London. Nothing at all, anywhere."

Dame Vivienne Westwood
(1941–2022)

Big Ben

BEST FOR: TICKING OFF THE BUCKET LIST
AREA: CITY OF WESTMINSTER

Don't Miss... The clock tower
when it's illuminated at night.

Did You Know... The monument was
officially renamed "Elizabeth Tower" in 2012
to honour the late Queen's Diamond Jubilee.

Insider Tip... There are 334 steps inside
the clock, so wear comfy shoes.

Big Ben needs no introduction. A cultural icon and a British institution, the clock tower at the Houses of Parliament is a must-see attraction, particularly on the hour when the loud chimes ring out across London.

"Big Ben" is actually the name given to the enormous 13-ton bell inside, and not the tower itself. However few Londoners have ever known the landmark by any other name since it was unveiled in 1856.

The attraction is so popular that, aside from taking in its staggering size from the ground, tickets to see the inner workings are released – and quickly snapped up – months in advance.

London's Burning

In 1666, a catastrophic fire swept through London and changed it forever.

The Great Fire of London started in a bakery on Pudding Lane near London Bridge and burned for four days straight, eventually reaching the Tower of London to the east and totally destroying St Paul's Cathedral to the west.

Today, to walk its path of destruction takes almost two hours. At every turn, there is a mixture between old London, with its narrow streets, and the more modern city, which took almost 50 years to plan and rebuild.

The 202-ft (62.5-m) high monument to commemorate the Great Fire is located on Fish Street Hill. Climb the 311 steps for views of the city.

The Great Fire of London by Numbers

❋ The fire sparked around **1 am** on **2 September 1666**

❋ It affected **80 per cent** of the city

❋ **30 navy soldiers** and **100 local volunteers** fought the blaze – the London Fire Brigade didn't exist

❋ The final fire was contained on **6 September**

❋ Only **6 deaths** were officially recorded, but it was thought to be hundreds more

❋ **13,200 houses** and **87 churches** were destroyed

❋ Thousands of people were left **homeless**

❋ The price of rebuilding the city was **£10 million** ($12 million) – about £2 billion today

❋ St Paul's was rebuilt in **1711**

Best Green Spaces

Primrose Hill
For spectacular London views

The Hill Garden and Pergola
(Hampstead Heath)
An oasis of peace and quiet

Isabella Plantation (Richmond Park)
Escape the city for woodland walks

Red Cross Garden (Southwark)
A central secret spot

Story Garden (Kings Cross)
Impressive eco-community

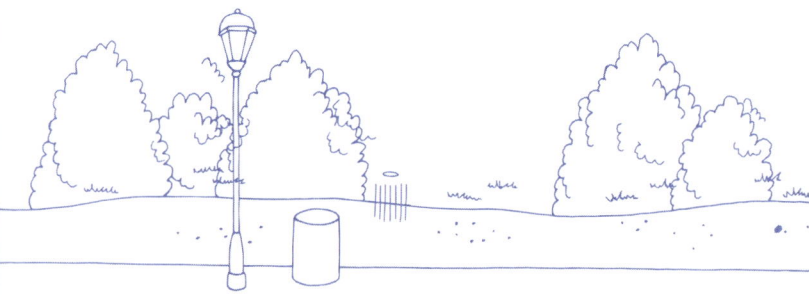

St James's Park (Westminster)
Across the road from the Palace

Chiswick House & Gardens (Chiswick)
For Palladian splendour

Chelsea Physic Garden (Chelsea)
Botanical bliss amongst rich history

Royal Botanic Gardens (Kew)
For vast landscapes and architecture

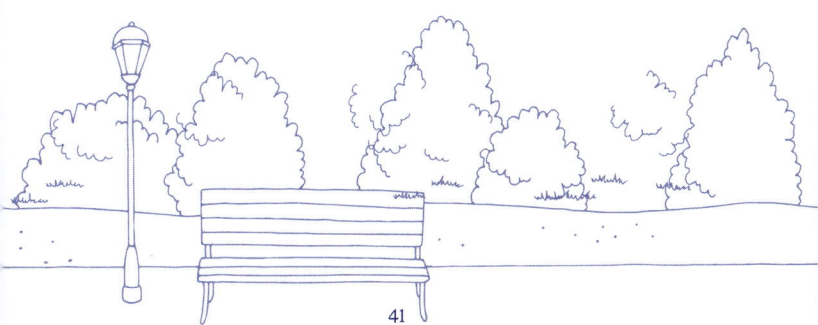

"The parks be the lungs of London."

Charles Dickens, *Sketches by Boz* (1836)

Did You Know?

London has so many trees it can technically be classed as a forest.

The largest of the capital's green spaces is Richmond Park, covering 2,500 acres and home to around 650 red and fallow deer.

The All England Lawn Tennis & Croquet Club

BEST FOR: TENNIS LOVERS
AREA: WIMBLEDON

A Mecca for sports fans, Wimbledon has a special place in the heart of Londoners. The All England Lawn Tennis & Croquet Club is home to one of the four Grand Slam competitions, and, even if you're not fortunate enough to get tickets, an off-season tour of the grounds is an unmissable chance to relive tennis history.

Each year at the Wimbledon Tennis Championships, spectators get through an incredible 166,000 servings of strawberries each year. In England, they symbolize the start of summer.

Hampton Court

BEST FOR: HISTORY LOVERS
AREA: RICHMOND

A half-hour train ride from central London lies Henry VIII's sprawling baroque palace.

Said to be his favourite residence out of the 60 he owned, the infamous Tudor king made vast improvements on what was once a modest abode.

With too many jewels to mention, a choice few must-sees include: the hammerbeam roof of the Great Hall, the huge roasting hearth in the kitchen, intricate murals on the King's Stairs and the ornate sunken gardens. Don't forget to look up – and marvel at the intricately designed brick chimneys.

Children will love the Magic Gardens – full of battlements to climb, mythical beasts to conquer, hills to roll down and plenty of water play.

CHAPTER TWO

MUSEUMS & GALLERIES

V&A Museum

BEST FOR: ART LOVERS
AREA: SOUTH KENSINGTON

Don't Miss... The foundation stone laid by Queen Victoria, just left of the main entrance.

Did You Know... This was the first museum to open a public restaurant.

Insider Tip... Look out for the oldest photographs of London, taken in 1839.

In every sense, the V&A's foundations were laid by Queen Victoria.

It was the brainchild of her beloved husband Prince Albert, who wanted to create a "cultural district" of museums in South Kensington. The queen put the last stone in its walls on completion, when it was renamed after the two of them in 1899.

It is not, as you might expect, dedicated to the lives of Victoria and Albert. The V&A is the world's largest museum of art and design; and it's seven miles of galleries offer a full day's worth of enjoyment.

Tate Modern

BEST FOR: CONTEMPORARY ART
AREA: BANKSIDE

Don't Miss... The 360-degree viewing tower on the tenth floor.

Did You Know... The man who donated the first contemporary paintings (and his last name) to the Tate galleries also introduced sugar cubes to the UK.

Insider Tip... Afternoon Tea on Level 6 is served with an incredible panoramic view of St Paul's.

Pablo Picasso, Salvador Dalí, Andy Warhol, Roy Lichtenstein: just a few of the artists whose collections are proudly on display at Tate Modern.

Since opening in 2000, the gallery has established itself as a world-leading institution of art, particularly for showcasing iconic works of the last century, including Warhol's *Marilyn Diptych* (1962) and Picasso's *The Three Dancers* (1925).

Combine a visit with a stroll along the South Bank for a truly inspirational afternoon.

British Museum

BEST FOR: CURIOUS MINDS
AREA: BLOOMSBURY

Don't Miss... The Rosetta Stone, the key that unlocked Egyptian hieroglyphics.

Did You Know... This museum once had its own dedicated Tube stop, but it was demolished after Holborn station opened.

Insider Tip... Book a time slot for the busiest exhibitions to avoid disappointment.

Decades ahead of its time, the British Museum was the first national museum to showcase all fields of human knowledge: from books to plant specimens, alongside historical objects such as candle holders and coins.

Originally, the contents was the private collection of one curious and well-travelled man, Sir Hans Sloane.

When the artefacts were purchased by King George II in 1753, they were used to create a public exhibition which today serves as a wonderland for curious minds, helping to piece together small pieces of history into one large portrait of the world.

Sherlock Holmes Museum

BEST FOR: BOOK WORMS
AREA: MARYLEBONE

Don't Miss... A souvenir shop boasting the largest selection of Sherlock memorabilia anywhere.

Did You Know... The author's writing chair sits inside this reimagined home.

Insider Tip... Buy your tickets in the gift shop before joining the queue.

There are many walking tours of London
that will tell you the stories of the city in
times gone by, but the Sherlock Holmes
Museum will transport you right back
to candle-lit Victorian London.

A tour of the authentic four-storey Georgian
townhouse takes you inside the real 221B
Baker Street – where many of Sir Arthur
Conan Doyle's famous tales began.

Fans will love the commemorative
blue plaque above the front door,
honouring a literary hero.

Literary London

Blue plaques to authors, poets
and writers of the city

Oscar Wilde (1854–1900) 34 Tite Street, Chelsea

Virginia Woolf (1882–1941) 29 Fitzroy Square,
Fitzrovia

Charles Dickens (1812–1870) 48 Doughty
Street, Holborn

T.S. Eliot (1888–1965) 3 Kensington Court
Gardens, Kensington

Samuel Pepys (1633–1703) 12 Buckingham
Street, Strand

Geoffrey Chaucer (1343–1400) The Tabard Inn,
Southwark

Dame Agatha Christie (1890–1976) 58 Sheffield
Terrace, Holland Park

Mary Shelley (1797–1851) 24 Chester Square,
Belgravia

Sylvia Plath (1932–1963) 3 Chalcot Square,
Primrose Hill

"To walk alone in London is the greatest rest."

Virginia Woolf, *Street Haunting* (1930)

Natural History Museum

**BEST FOR: HISTORY OF LIFE ON EARTH
AREA: SOUTH KENSINGTON**

Don't Miss... The enormous 82-ft (25.2-m) long skeleton of a blue whale looming over Hintze Hall.

Did You Know... The museum offers more relaxed sessions for neurodivergent visitors.

Insider Tip... The V&A and the Science Museum are just around the corner.

There has never been a generation more interested in – or protective of – Planet Earth. That might explain why visitor numbers are increasing year on year, nearly a century and a half after it was founded.

It is a fascinating place for adults and children alike – with jaw-dropping skeletons of dinosaurs, impressive fossil collections and a range of interactive exhibits.

Not only is the museum showcasing the history of our natural world, but there is a large focus on preserving it, with scientists actively working on-site to advance our knowledge.

Did You Know?

London black cab drivers
(cabbies) need to memorize
every street name in London
to pass the legendary test, the
Knowledge. It's said to take
around three years to learn!

The iconic black cab's proper name
is the Hackney Carriage, stemming
from the times that private
horse and carts would transport
people around the capital.

Must-see Monuments & Statues

Battle of Britain Monument (Victoria Embankment)
Remembering those who lost their life in World War II's Battle of Britain

The Lions (Trafalgar Square)
Four bronze lions surround Nelson's Column, representing the Admiral's heroism

Cleopatra's Needle (Victoria Embankment)
This ancient obelisk was gifted to Britain by the Sultan of Egypt and Sudan in 1878

Diana, Princess of Wales Memorial Fountain (Hyde Park)
Both sculpture and water feature, the oval shape has three bridges to cross

Peter Pan statue (Kensington Gardens)
The bronze boy that never grows up is surrounded by intricate animals

The Cenotaph (Whitehall)
The focal point of Britain's Remembrance Day parade, dedicated to "the glorious dead"

CHAPTER THREE

SHOPPING

Harrods

BEST FOR: BIG SPENDING
AREA: KNIGHTSBRIDGE

Don't Miss... The 12,000 dazzling bulbs that put Harrods' name in lights during the festive season.

Did You Know... This store was the first place in England to have an escalator inside.

Insider Tip... There is a dress code that prohibits ripped jeans and flip flops.

Anything that you could possibly need or desire, Harrods has it. Over 100,000 pairs of shoes on the fifth floor. Fine watches and fine wines. Its own bureau de change, blow-dry bar, pharmacy and wellness spa. At one time, Harrods even had a zoo.

Whole afternoons could be spent in this 5-acre mini city, with so much more to see inside than fashion.

Look out for cut-glass chandeliers, baroque architecture and lovingly restored Edwardian details, as well as a marble memorial to Harrods employees who never came back from World War I.

Hamleys

BEST FOR: CHILDREN
AREA: REGENT STREET

Don't Miss... A collector's favourite:
Hamleys teddy bears.

Did You Know... Queen Elizabeth II used to
buy Hamleys toys for her own children.

Insider Tip... If you arrive at opening time,
go straight to the top floor – where it will
be quietest – and work your way down.

Promising fun on every floor, Hamleys is a shopping experience that children – and the young-at-heart – simply should not miss.

Follow in the footsteps of British royalty, who have shopped at the world's largest toy emporium for birthday and Christmas presents for over two centuries.

It's an afternoon of total escapism, as bubbles and live performers on the door will have you dancing in the streets before you've even entered.

Inside, in among seven storeys of the world's finest toys, is an ice-cream parlour and games arcade, ideal for entertaining London's tiniest tourists.

Best Play Parks near Shopping Destinations

Diana, Princess of Wales Memorial Playground (near Kensington High Street)
For scenic surrounds

Biodiversity Playground
(near Westfield Stratford City)
To blow off steam

Wembley Park (near London Designer Outlet)
For a wet weather run-around

Battersea Park Playground
(near Battersea Power Station)
For all-age fun

Gloucester Gate Playground
(near Camden Market)
For sand and water play

"Put your walking shoes on, set off without any plan and don't be afraid of getting lost."

America Ferrera, *The Standard*, 10 April 2012

Oxford Street

BEST FOR: SHOPPING 'TIL YOU DROP
AREA: CITY OF WESTMINSTER

Don't Miss... Regent Street and Carnaby Street nearby.

Did You Know... Oxford Street features on the British Monopoly board.

Insider Tip... Avoid Oxford Street Tube station during commuter times. Walk from Bond Street or Tottenham Court Road stations instead.

The world's biggest high street covers
three Tube stations and a walking distance
of 1.5 miles (2.4 km) – and that's not counting
square footage inside every fashion store
imaginable along its well-trodden parade.

Oxford Street is home to 90 flagship
stores, including John Lewis, Selfridges
and Kurt Geiger, as well as over 500
nearby restaurants, making it the ultimate
shopping destination in the British capital.

At Christmas, around 300,000 lights
dangle above shoppers, and the stores
stay open later into the evening.

Where to Shop at Christmas

Covent Garden is the ultimate festive fashion destination in the west end

Start with...

Honey butter toast and hot chocolate from Arôme Bakery in the heart of Covent Garden to fuel your festive treasure hunt.

Shop for...

Everything from designer goods at Chanel and Tom Ford to luxury stocking fillers from Jo Malone and Molton Brown.

Rock around...

The iconic 60-ft (18-m) Covent Garden Christmas Tree, next to Market Building, where "snow" falls every day from 12–9 pm.

Stop for...

Lunch on the balcony at Dolce VyTA overlooking the piazza, and make your shopping hit list for the afternoon.

Don't miss...

St Martin's Courtyard, Floral Court and Long Acre for over 100 fashion brands, like Zara, Jaeger, Barbour and AllSaints.

Wander to...

The bustling Christmas market in Leicester Square, just six minutes' walk away, for a fun atmosphere and unique festive gift ideas.

Get merry with...

Cocktails at LSQ Rooftop, as a mirage of spectacular Christmas lights switch on across London's skyline.

Portobello Road Market

BEST FOR: VINTAGE TREASURES
AREA: NOTTING HILL

Don't Miss... One of London's oldest and most famous pubs, The Churchill Arms, which is always heavily adorned with flowers.

Did You Know... Just around the corner is The Notting Hill Bookshop, which was recreated for the 1999 film, *Notting Hill.*

Insider Tip... The famous food market, selling organic produce, baked goods and seafood, runs on Saturday mornings.

The old English charm of Notting Hill is at
its peak when the full street market rolls
out on Portobello Road at weekends.

What started as a humble open-air market
around 150 years ago has become one of the
UK's most popular shopping experiences,
and remains a genuine slice of London life.

The best treasure hunting takes place
on Fridays, with vintage clothing and
accessories stalls on offer, and Saturdays,
when the antiques arcade opens.

If you find a seat at one of the many
cafés, this buzzing high street is
a people watcher's paradise.

Did You Know?

Almost 200 festivals take place
in London every year.

One of the world's most famous,
Notting Hill Carnival, takes
over the affluent West London
neighbourhood for one weekend
every summer, and attracts roughly
two million spirited revellers.

"Behind everything in London is something else, and, behind that, is something else still; and so on through the centuries, so that London as we see her is only the latest manifestation of other Londons, and to love her is to plunge into ancestor-worship."

H.V. Morton, *In Search of London* (1951)

Knightsbridge

BEST FOR: DESIGNER FASHION
AREA: KNIGHTSBRIDGE

Don't Miss... The decadent window displays, especially at Christmas.

Did You Know... Apartments in the area sell for over £100 million ($125 million).

Insider Tip... You can see lots more if you explore the area by bus than Tube-hopping on the Underground.

From Hermès to Valentino and the world-famous designer emporium Harvey Nichols, every fashion brand imaginable can be found in upmarket Knightsbridge.

It's where global stars, models and media moguls come to pick up the very latest trends, without a care for the price tag. With luxury supercars on every corner, this neighbourhood is not only a place to see, but to be seen.

Make time for a wander through Hyde Park, Knightsbridge's 142-hectare back garden.

Did You Know?

Shortly after recording their first studio album, *Please Please Me*, in 1963, the Beatles moved into a top-floor flat, just off the corner of Hyde Park, on 57 Green Street.

It's the only home all four ever shared together.

Best Bookshops

Daunt Books (Marylebone)
Browse in beautiful surrounds

London Review of Books (Brick Lane)
Modern and chic

Foyles (Charing Cross)
An impressive selection

Stanfords (Covent Garden)
A travel treasure trove

Hatchards (Piccadilly)
The UK'S oldest bookshop

John Sandoe (Chelsea)
Straight out of a Dickens novel

Gosh! Comics (Soho)
Graphic novel heaven

CHAPTER FOUR

FOOD & DRINK

Afternoon Tea at the Ritz

BEST FOR: A LUXURY EXPERIENCE
AREA: MAYFAIR

Don't Miss... Children's afternoon tea for special family occasions.

Did You Know... One corridor was specifically designed for two ladies wearing voluminous dresses to walk comfortably side by side.

Insider Tip... Avoid jeans, shorts, trainers and sportswear to stick to the elegant dress code of this five-star establishment.

The quintessential British afternoon tea features a mouth-watering combination of delicate finger sandwiches, cakes, and scones with cream and jam. All served alongside a pot of piping hot tea; and sometimes even champagne.

In London, there's nowhere more famous to enjoy this fashionable custom than the Ritz. After all, it was the first hotel to welcome ladies to share afternoon tea without male company.

It was, and still is, quite the social occasion, now accompanied by a live pianist and offering a choice of 18 of the finest loose-leaf teas.

A Great British Tradition

Loved by royals and Londoners alike since 1840

Afternoon tea was invented as an elegant solution to the slump between lunch and dinner, and was the idea of the late Duchess of Bedford, Anna Russell – a close friend of Queen Victoria. When hunger struck, the Duchess would request a tray of sandwiches, cakes and tea to tide her over.

The Queen took fondly to the idea, and began inviting high-society friends to enjoy it with her. It is well known that her great-great-granddaughter, Queen Elizabeth II, enjoyed afternoon tea every day, wherever she was in the world.

"When a man is tired of London, he is tired of life."

Samuel Johnson, September 1777

Sunday Roast at the Engineer

BEST FOR: TRADITIONAL PUB GRUB
AREA: PRIMROSE HILL

Don't Miss... The much-loved dessert options.

Did You Know... Their food
menu changes daily.

Insider Tip... The secret garden terrace
is heated and rain-proof, so don't let the
weather put you off eating al fresco.

What better way to end a stroll in Regent's Park than with a roast dinner with all the trimmings? It's what the English consider a cozy Sunday.

Step into a quaint villagey pub a stone's throw from Primrose Hill, where the jaw-dropping views of the capital city are the only reminder you're still in London.

Loyal locals love this relaxed eatery, which feels more like a home-from-home than a top-rated restaurant.

Don't miss the beer garden at the back, which patrons like to think of as their own little secret.

Fine Dining at Heron Tower

BEST FOR: ROMANCE
AREA: BISHOPSGATE

Don't Miss... The signature Duck
& Waffle dish, which is requested
around 7,000 times a month.

Did You Know... This is the restaurant
that never sleeps. It is open 24 hours.

Insider Tip... Online reservations
open two months in advance (but call
directly to ask about cancellations).

When it comes to fancy food with a view, you are spoilt for choice with London skyscrapers.

There's Aqua, up 31 floors, at The Shard or Fenchurch restaurant inside London's highest public garden at the Walkie Talkie (aka the Fenchurch Building). Then there's OXO Tower Restaurant, one of the first to take dining to new heights.

The highest and arguably finest is an unbelievable 574 ft (174 m) above the City at Heron Tower. Duck & Waffle has held the top spot for high-flying dining since 2012, thanks in part to its namesake sweet and savoury dish, but also for the incredible lift that shoots to the 40th floor in seconds.

Full English Breakfast at the Regency Café

BEST FOR: A GREAT WAKE-UP
AREA: WESTMINSTER

Don't Miss... The tasty English 18th-century staple, bubble & squeak, to order with your set breakfast.

Did You Know... A family of four looking for a hearty start can eat well for under £30 ($37).

Insider Tip... Don't be put off by the queue – it moves quickly.

Popular with those who know the city better than anyone – London's black cab drivers – the Regency Café often has hungry foodies queueing out the door for a traditional no-frills fry-up.

This charming café has all the ingredients for a "Full English" experience, including authentic retro décor and friendly service.

Since opening in 1946, it has featured in Hollywood films such as *Layer Cake*, though one reason for its popularity is that you can still get a generous portion of great quality food at a fair price. Just like old times.

Street Food at Borough Market

**BEST FOR: A TASTE ADVENTURE
AREA: LONDON BRIDGE**

Don't Miss... Out on a good thing just because of a long line. Prepare to queue for the very best of Borough Market.

Did You Know... The market has only been open on Sundays since 2021.

Insider Tip... Avoid Mondays and Tuesdays when the market is partially closed.

Bring your heartiest appetite
to an historic food market one
thousand years in the making.

Borough Market, set in the heart of
south-east London, has more than
100 food stalls, stands and restaurants
offering a melting pot of British
and international cuisines.

It's best to go without a plan and see
where your taste buds take you.

However, seasoned foodies will tell you
to try a comforting cheese toastie at
Kappacasein and the famous stuffed
dumplings from Juma, called "kubba".

CHAPTER FIVE

MUSIC & CULTURE

Royal Ballet & Opera

BEST FOR: BALLET OR OPERA
AREA: COVENT GARDEN

Don't Miss... Free events sign-posted on the official website.

Did You Know... The grand staircase in the foyer was made wide enough to cater for ladies' fashion of the 1800s.

Insider Tip... Ask ushers for a cushion if your view of the stage is obstructed.

To many visitors of London, it will always be known as the Royal Opera House. In 2024, the Covent Garden landmark changed its name to include "Ballet" and drop "House".

The Royal Ballet and Opera has been the collective home of The Royal Ballet company and The Royal Opera since 1858. To admirers of the arts, it would seem there has never been anywhere else for it in London.

First-timers shouldn't be put off by pomp and pageantry. Prices for shows vary widely to ensure that the arts are accessible – and welcoming – to everyone.

The Top Secret Comedy Club

BEST FOR: STAND-UP
AREA: COVENT GARDEN

Don't Miss... Cheap pre-show
drinks at the bar.

Did You Know... When comics sell out sets,
sometimes they will perform both upstairs
and downstairs on the same night.

Insider Tip... On selected nights,
tickets can be as cheap as £1 ($1.25).

If you love the British sense of humour, a comedy night in the capital will definitely put a smile on your face.

The Top Secret Comedy Club is the most popular venue in London for laughs, where an inexpensive bar and reasonably priced tickets only add to the appeal.

Shows regularly feature surprise appearances from celebrity stand-ups excited to try out new material on unsuspecting audiences.

Some of the venue's biggest supporters include Jack Whitehall and Trevor Noah.

The Globe Theatre

BEST FOR: SHAKESPEARE ON STAGE
AREA: SOUTHWARK

Don't Miss... An indoor theatre just inside called the Sam Wanamaker Playhouse.

Did You Know... It's the only building in the city with a thatched roof, as they were banned after the Great Fire of London.

Insider Tip... Best views of the stage are often standing tickets, which used to be sold for a penny in Shakespearean times.

To take in a show at the Globe Theatre is to experience theatre in the way Shakespeare's generation would have: intimate, unfiltered and often in the worst of English weather.

The open-air theatre is a reimagining of the original – built by Shakespeare's own theatre company – after it was destroyed by fire from a rogue theatrical cannon in 1613.

Not only is it your chance to see the bard's famous works on stage, but the guided tours are a great way to learn more about a playwright synonymous with London.

Ronnie Scott's Jazz Club

BEST FOR: WORLD-FAMOUS JAZZ
AREA: SOHO

Don't Miss... The tables right at the front – the experience is unrivalled.

Did You Know... This was the music venue for Jimi Hendrix's last public appearance in 1970.

Insider Tip... Mobile phones are banned inside, so this is not the place for selfies.

On any night of the week, Ronnie Scott's is packed full of ardent jazz fans.

The venue is dimly lit, intimate and electric with atmosphere, so even after 65 years, bagging one of the 200 seats still feels likes the hottest ticket in town.

It was started by the saxophonist of the same name, who was inspired to open the UK's first modern jazz club after visiting Manhattan's legendary 52nd Street.

You name it, they have played at this renowned club, from Miles Davies to Ella Fitzgerald.

Shaftesbury Avenue

BEST FOR: MUSICALS
AREA: LEICESTER SQUARE

Don't Miss... Matinee or week-night performances are often the quietest shows at the most affordable prices.

Did You Know... You can purchase last-minute standby or returned tickets directly from theatre box offices.

Insider Tip... Examine seating plans before purchasing to make sure you secure unobstructed seats.

By day, Shaftesbury Avenue screams the names of its biggest-selling shows from electric billboards.

By night, the West End is alive with the sound of their music, whether it's blaring out from passing rickshaws or theatregoers spilling onto the street singing show tunes.

This legendary district holds an array of theatre records: the oldest London theatre – Lyric Theatre – opened in 1888, and the largest – Apollo Victoria – seating 2,381 theatregoers.

It's also home to the unbeatable *Harry Potter and the Cursed Child*, which has won nine Olivier Awards since opening in 2016.

Did You Know?

There's a special reason why
J.K. Rowling chose London's
Kings Cross station to take
Harry to Hogwarts.

The author's parents actually met
here, on a train bound for Scotland.

Warner Bros Studio London: The Making of Harry Potter

BEST FOR: POTTERHEADS
AREA: WATFORD

In London, magic is only a short ride away! Harry Potter fans couldn't possibly come this close to the Wizarding World without boarding their own "Knight Bus" of-sorts to the action.

Included within the Harry Potter Studio Tour ticket price is the 20-minute train journey from Euston station.

Don't miss... Platform 9¾ at London King's Cross station for a photo with the luggage trolley stuck in the wall (but expect to queue!).

CHAPTER SIX

NIGHT LIFE

Cahoots

BEST FOR: AN IMMERSIVE EXPERIENCE
AREA: SOHO

Don't Miss... The Vera Lynn cocktail.

Did You Know... The basement venue was used as an air raid shelter during World War II.

Insider Tip... There is an option for bottomless cocktails.

Inspired by the 40 lost or forgotten London Underground stations, this place is open for time travel.

Though this Tube stop is fictional, you'd never know it. Go deep beneath the city via wooden escalators, eerily reminiscent of a bygone era, and hop on a vintage train decorated with authentic moquette seats.

Those who come for the seriously popular cocktails will leave with a great taste of 1940s London.

The Tube

The world's first underground railway

* More than **1 billion** passengers travel on the London Underground every year

* Londoners call it the **"Tube"**

* It is the world's oldest network, and opened in **1863**

* Today, it covers more than **250 miles** (402 km) of track, and has **11 lines** and **272 stops**

* The new **Elizabeth Line** (opened in 2023) is not technically considered part of the London Underground

* Only **45 per cent** of the tracks are actually underground

Did You Know?

East London was one of the areas worst affected by bombing during World War II.

At the height of the Blitz – an eight-month air raid attack on Britain in 1940 – the capital was bombed for 57 nights in a row and the Underground stations were used for shelter.

KOKO

BEST FOR: LIVE MUSIC
AREA: CAMDEN

Don't Miss... The mesmerizing disco ball hanging above the dance floor.

Did You Know... The venue recently reopened after a seven-year £70 million ($87 million) refurbishment.

Insider Tip... Inside the venue there are a select few secret spaces, including listening booths for playing your favourite vinyl albums in private.

If you have come to Camden Town, you will no doubt be looking for something cool. And, whether you want club nights or live music, the iconic KOKO delivers every time.

The venue opened as a theatre at the turn of the last century, and maintains its Victorian charm – with balcony boxes and an expansive dance floor that was once lined with seats. All in all, it's a quirky place to see electronic music, DJ sets or hip-hop acts.

Madonna, Prince, Amy Winehouse, and the Rolling Stones have all played here, so it's often the place to catch world-famous performers.

The London Cabaret Club

BEST FOR: SPECIAL OCCASIONS
AREA: HOLBORN

Don't Miss... The dazzling show outfits.

Did You Know... Around 300 performers audition to be in each new show at this club.

Insider Tip... For a daytime alternative, look out for their bottomless brunch events.

This unique night out puts an exotic
spin on the traditional "dinner
and a show" in London.

When the London Cabaret Club first
came to the city as a pop-up, there was
so much demand for more shows that
they had to find a permanent residence.
And what better place than the decadent
Bloomsbury Ballroom inside a Grade
II-listed art deco 1920s building.

An evening of exceptional live
performances and fine dining awaits,
all with a classically British theme.

Village

BEST FOR: LGBTQIA+ NIGHTS
AREA: SOHO

Don't Miss... Happy hour.

Did You Know... There are more gay bars in Soho per square mile than any other London area.

Insider Tip... Come for relaxed drinks in the Café Bar. Stay for dancing in the basement.

Now Soho's longest-serving gay bar,
legendary venue Village seems
to get better with age.

If it weren't for the neon rainbows and
flags flying high outside, this small corner
pub might seem unassuming. Inside, it's
deceptively large, spread over three floors,
with rooms to suit different moods.

Many come in the early evening for 2-for-
1 cocktails and stay for karaoke, only to
find themselves dancing downstairs until
the early hours. This welcoming "village"
feel keeps punters coming back.

Soho

The spiritual home of the LGBTQIA+ community

At the turn of the 19th century, the area around Piccadilly Circus became a hub for art, theatre and decadence. This included a lively gay-friendly scene, with institutions such as the Caravan Club and the Trocadero Long Bar opening their doors.

In the first half of the 20th century, police regularly raided these West End gay venues, which were an open secret among locals, driving the queer community underground.

It wasn't until the 1950s that the scene began to emerge once again, and by the late 1970s Soho had fully embraced its status as the epicentre of Queer London. Gay bars, burlesque clubs and sex shops proudly popped up, and still remain.

Guide to Pride

One event not to be missed is Pride In London, which takes over the city for the month of June. The annual celebration is dedicated to highlighting, supporting and advancing LGBTQIA+ rights.

Ways to celebrate...

✳ March in the parade from Hyde Park Corner to Whitehall

✳ Wear bold colours – as loud as possible!

✳ Visit the UK's first LGBTQIA+ museum, Queer Britain

✳ Attend free performances in Trafalgar Square

✳ Enjoy a drag show, musical or cabaret performance

✳ Visit the UK's first dedicated LGBTQIA+ bookstore, Gay's The Word

Ministry of Sound

**BEST FOR: CLUB NIGHTS
AREA: ELEPHANT & CASTLE**

Don't Miss... The advance tickets, which are slightly cheaper than on the door.

Did You Know... Ministry of Sound opened quietly in 1991, giving it the allure of a well-kept secret that – pretty soon – everyone wanted to know.

Insider Tip... Go VIP for a little extra attention.

Ministry of Sound put London on the map for dance music, launching in the 1990s with the best sound system in town. At the time, the venue didn't even have a licence to serve alcohol, but it was so popular that it emptied out every rival super-club during its opening six months.

Its club nights are so legendary they still attract thousands of revellers every weekend.

Dance lovers will make pilgrimages from all across the country just to see world-class DJs play, some of whom have been here ever since it opened in 1991.

A Tale of Two Stations

Why so near? St Pancras and Kings Cross

There's a reason why two of London's busiest railway stations were built over the road from one another... it's beer.

London St Pancras International (as it's now known) was built in 1868 – just 16 years after, and a stone's throw away from, King's Cross – as a faster and more cost-effective solution for transporting thousands of barrels of Staffordshire ale to the UK's beer-loving capital.

The stations are so close that, today, they're served by the same Underground stop: King's Cross St Pancras.

Must-Visit Pubs

Ye Olde Cheshire Cheese (Holborn)
Revel in the history

The Audley Public House (Mayfair)
For a posh pint

The Royal Oak (Marylebone)
For British grub

The Harp (Covent Garden)
Popular and buzzy

The Duke of Edinburgh (Brixton)
Visit for the beer garden

The Cross Keys (Covent Garden)
Best value you'll find so centrally

"London is a city of endless possibility and endless charm."

Bill Bryson,
Notes from a Small Island (1995)